CREATIVE WRITING EXERCISES

IMPROVE YOUR CRAFT THROUGH PLAY

MARK BOUTROS

Copyright © 2025 by Mark Boutros

All rights reserved.

No part of this book may be reproduced in any form or by any electronic or mechanical means, including information storage and retrieval systems, without written permission from the author, except for the use of brief quotations in a book review.

NO AI TRAINING: Without in any way limiting the author's exclusive rights under copyright, any use of this publication to 'train' generative artificial intelligence (AI) technologies to generate text is expressly prohibited. The author reserves all rights to licence uses of this work for generative AI training and development of machine learning language models.

Cover designed by: Bobby Birchall at Bobby&Co

Edited by: Christelle Roy-Corbin

This book is written in UK English.

Print ISBN: 978-1-9191840-0-5

 Formatted with Vellum

For my writing students who approach these exercises with enthusiasm and humour, and who teach me more than I likely teach them.
Keep doing what you do.

CONTENTS

Introduction	ix

CREATING IDEAS
What if I wasn't distracted?	5
Loglines from titles	9
What's going on?	11
Newsworthy	13
Genre shift	16
Out of thin air	18
I want	20
The worst ideas	22
Tips	24

CHARACTER AND MOTIVATION
Opposites	29
Character from a logline	32
Build a life	35
What would you do?	37
Letter from your protagonist	40
Secondary characters	44
Quotes	46
Represent	48
Peace talks	51
First impressions	53
Humanise it	55
Flip it	57
Bad to the bone	59
Argue with yourself	61
Tips	63

STORY WORLD
What happened here?	67
What do I see?	69
Adventure time	71

If it was a person	73
Soundtrack to the scene	75
Tips	77

STRUCTURE

Beginning, middle, and end	81
Who do I become?	85
It starts with the end	87
Break it down	89
The blank page	91
Improve it	93
Whose fault is it anyway?	96
Tag team	98
Draw the poster	102
Story corner	104
Tips	106

RAISE THE STAKES

The worst thing that can happen	111
Give it meaning	113
The power of the inciting incident	115
The clock is ticking	117
Up the drama	121
But it's boring	124
Tips	126

TECHNIQUE AND GENERAL

Decluttering	131
Activate	133
Add essence	136
Subtext	139
Only action	142
Blurb it out	143
Exposition	145
Cliché away	147
Tips	149

THE WRITER'S MIND

What's the best that can happen?	153
Letter to yourself	155

No to your notes	157
I love writing because…	159
I'm allowed to…	160
Make a vow	162
What's stopping me?	164
Tips	166

THE FINAL CHALLENGE

Your time to shine	171
Bibliography	173
Acknowledgments	177
About the Author	179

INTRODUCTION

Hello,

I'm Mark, a UK based, International Emmy nominated TV writer, hybrid author, and screenwriting teacher. I've written professionally for over 20 years, and in that time I've won competitions, lost others, had scripts commissioned and aired on TV, and seen plenty go nowhere. Like the stories we share, a writing career has an ebb and flow, ups and downs, twists and turns, and we evolve through the journey.

This evolution is why I'm writing this book. For some time, my thinking was rigid, focused purely on structure, and I needed to reintroduce myself to my inner child to prioritise play and creativity over function and form.

I have the privilege of working with writers at multiple universities: NYU London and the London Film School where I teach film, and I spent near a decade at the Central School of Speech and Drama teaching TV writing. I've also taught at the University of Roehampton, and delivered creative writing sessions for the Games Workshop and Cambridge University. Before that, I was a TV producer, and I still write for television to keep my teaching relevant. I also worked at Google for a year, writing dialogue and designing the personality for their Google Assistant. AI is not my fault.

I adore what I do, because I get to work with writers of all ages and backgrounds, and I'm around creativity, story, and humanity. It's taught me that we all have a process, and that can be healthy for a while, but can become a hindrance. Like our characters, we need to acknowledge our flaws, our habits, and welcome new ways of doing things to truly evolve. That's what this book is about, reconnecting with the playful side of yourself to create ideas you care about, to solve problems in existing stories you're writing, and to improve your craft through play.

This book is for you if:

- You want to shake up your process.
- You're seeking inspiration.
- You want to embrace the playful side of writing.
- You need help to get unstuck during certain story points.
- You want to practice without pressure.
- You want specific techniques to address weaknesses in your writing.

A lot of writers dismiss creative writing exercises, because yes, they can feel childish, but that's the point. Sometimes we need to reconnect with that inner-child, and resistance can be a signal. It's often fear of the unfamiliar and us wanting to stay stuck in our mindset. If something in this book annoys you, take a breath and sit with the feeling. Maybe it is me that's annoying, but maybe it's discomfort, and that's worth exploring, as that's where growth lives.

Why play matters:

Creation is meant to be joyful. Play increases our capacity for ideas, allows us to fail, and takes the pressure off. For those of us with writing anxiety, it also gets us out of our own way.

Structure has become the word of the day with so much of storytelling, but it can turn us into story mathematicians rather than creatives. Creativity happens in freedom. Structural constraints can come later, and we all have an inherent idea of structure from what we've consumed throughout our lives.

Dr. Stuart Brown, a doctor and psychiatrist who founded the National Institute for Play, has researched how play supports open-mindedness and adaptability, things that are essential to writing. His work also emphasises how play can improve emotional regulation and promote resilience. Both needed when writing!

Play also reduces self-criticism, as there are no stakes to it, it boosts idea creation due to the lack of limitations, focuses engagement, and can create emotional breakthroughs when something resonates with you.

How to use the book:

I've organised the book into chapters that address many topics including:

- Idea creation.
- Character and motivation.
- Story world.
- Structure.

Each section includes exercises and explains their usefulness as I've observed, and sometimes I will do the exercises to offer examples. I'll generally avoid doing so, as I don't want to influence your thinking.

Between chapters you'll find brief motivational interludes and writing advice. They're reminders that writing is emotional as well as technical.

You don't have to read in order. Use this book in a way that helps you to get the most out of it. Jump around or modify exercises to suit your needs. Try the ones you think might be pointless. They could surprise you and push you in a direction that awakens a new way of thinking.

What this book isn't:

An academic text. I'm writing purely from experience, which spans decades and over four thousand writing students. While I will reference some stories to give examples, this is not a deep dive into the history of writing and creativity.

I hope this book helps you. If you like it, please leave a review, as it will help others who may need it to discover it, and we all crave the algorithm doing us a favour. If you hate it, you're welcome to do the same, as it's important to be honest. My life will continue.

Happy writing!
Mark

CREATING IDEAS

We find ideas, or they find us in multiple ways. It could be a news story that triggers something. It could be a song lyric, a friend's anecdote, or a feeling we want to explore. However, sometimes, we're not sure where to start, and we're not sure how to turn an idea into a story.

Firstly, an idea becomes a story when a character has a problem to contend with. That's what creates momentum, stakes, and change. That's also where a lot of people get stuck. They have an idea, but they're not sure where to go next. It's where a logline can help. If you know what a logline is, skip ahead, otherwise read below, as a few exercises require you to use one.

Logline:
A short summary of your story. It covers the protagonist, the inciting incident, the antagonistic force, and your protagonist's action.

For example, this is from the TV comedy *30 Rock*:

The socially awkward head writer of a sketch comedy show must deal with an arrogant new boss and crazy new star, all while trying to run a successful show without losing her mind.

- **Protagonist:** Awkward head writer (female).
- **Inciting incident and antagonistic force:** New boss and crazy new star.
- **Action:** Having to keep things successful while dealing with them.

It implies stakes, which are her sanity and the success of the show, and it has an important detail, a description of the character: socially awkward.

That is often missing in a lot of loglines and prevents you getting deeper into character. It's often a flaw your protagonist needs to overcome, and something that holds them back and generates conflict. When you write a logline, make sure you think of that description. It is essential to create engagement, as it makes whatever your character does difficult. It also means whoever reads your logline asks questions and makes connections.

Another example, from the film *Finding Nemo*:

When his son is captured by divers, an anxious clownfish embarks on a perilous journey through the ocean to bring him back.

Again, you have everything you need. The who, the what, the why, and the implication of stakes. If you're lacking conflict in your logline, it's often because you lack a description for your character which is at odds with the situation. An anxious character being on a perilous journey gives us plenty of dramatic potential.

Also, as you can see, no names were used, because they're meaningless in a logline unless the story is about a real person.

I hope the upcoming exercises help. You'll likely enjoy some and hate others. Use what works for you and what gets you thinking.

WHAT IF I WASN'T DISTRACTED?

This is a well-known exercise that I approach slightly differently. It's best done alone, as it means you sit with your thoughts.

Your task:

Spend fifteen uninterrupted minutes writing a stream of "what if?" sentences. For example:

- What if my parents divorced and my dad moved in with me?
- What if the world had no music?
- What if a missing person reappeared after twenty years?

You should also follow these rules:

- Uninterrupted means no phones, no emails, no music. No distractions.
- If possible, write by hand in a notebook. It's slower and more meditative, but if you have particular

accessibility needs or would rather not use paper, then typing or voice notes will work fine.

At first, you'll write obvious and familiar material, but I want you to keep generating until you get to the weird and wonderful depths of your mind. **Do not self-edit.** Nobody else needs to ever see it!

Once you finish:

1. Read your list out loud.
2. Look for the ones that resonate. Maybe one, or maybe more stick out. It could be your next story.

Why this helps?

This frees your mind. I find when I do it I expose how much of a mess my brain is, but that's the point. Get into those depths. We're all weird, so own your weirdness, as that is also where uniqueness and wonder live. You might unearth an idea that is uniquely you and captures your voice.

This also builds a habit where you focus solely on one thing, and it can help you to become more present, which is valuable to take into your career as a writer.

What this could look like:

One idea could really take your attention: *What if I received a voicemail from my dead grandmother today?*

You feel like it's strong, so imagine what that looks like and write it: *My phone buzzes on my desk. A missed call from an unknown number and a voicemail. I press play, looking for a distrac-*

tion from reading a contract. It's her voice—hoarse, blunt—saying my name.

Already, your question has turned into the beginnings of a scene, the seed of a story. So keep going: *She tells me she's fine. That she forgives me. But I never asked for her forgiveness. Nor did I think I needed it.*

Once you're in the flow your subconscious will join you, giving you more than you expected. The "what if?" has just turned into an opportunity: *She continued. "Be careful around your mother..." Then the line goes dead.*

There you have tension, character, mystery, and suggestions of a genre and tone, all from a "what if?" You could leave it here, or keep pushing, taking us into the mystery. Who was grandma? What is wrong with the mother? What in our protagonist's life will be challenged through unravelling this mystery? How did the grandma contact her grandchild from the grave?

That's the beauty of this exercise. It can give you a fascinating spark that you can fan into a flame.

Variation if you're stuck on a scene/chapter:

It's normal to get stuck, and to lose grip on our characters and what we're trying to do. This normally happens at a scene/chapter level, where we don't know where to go next, or it can be at the planning stage in an outline.

The first thing I would do is ask these questions. Am I stuck because:

- The moment is not connected to theme?
- I don't know what my character would do?
- I don't know where the story is going?
- I've lost the emotional arc?

To help remedy the issue:

- Take the specific moment you are stuck at in your story.
- Spend ten uninterrupted minutes writing a stream of "what if?" sentences. For example: What if my character revealed they had an affair?

Follow the same rules as before, avoiding distractions. From this, you'll likely have a list of random nonsense, contrivances, and things that happen to, rather than things that happen because of your character.

Look at the list and read it out loud.

Does something resonate? Does something poke at you? Is there a flicker of hope there?

Most of the time the issue is with character, so if you still can't find a solution, go back to who they are and what the change they need to go through is. Sometimes the scene/chapter we're stuck on is the result of it not being emotionally connected to what they need to experience in order to change.

LOGLINES FROM TITLES

This solo or group exercise looks at how words trigger connections, and how a title can inspire story creation.

Your task:

Take three of the titles from the table coming up and write a logline for each of them.

Some writers like to rush, using their first thoughts, so I suggest taking at least twenty minutes to really think about this. By spending more time, you'll get deeper into the characters and story.

You want the logline to do the following:

- Communicate who the protagonist is.
- Tell us the inciting incident and the protagonist's action as a result of it.
- Imply stakes or directly state them.
- Identify the antagonistic force.

Why this helps?

Existing words can trigger thoughts and creativity. Sometimes we need that initial spark and these titles can provide it.

This'll help you to create new ideas, practice logline writing in a low stakes situation, and it'll make you focus on character, as loglines are about character and how everything links to them.

It'll also make you think about how titles suggest a particular entertainment experience. Maybe you'll want to write something that is clearly linked to the title, or maybe you'll want to be more abstract or surreal. Titles can suggest genre, tone, and many other things, so pay attention to your mind and maybe even ask why the title makes you create certain associations.

The titles:

Here are suggestions, but you can also come up with your own:

The Undertakers	The Stranger	Hope in the Hopeless
Frantic	The Way We Were	Old Boots
Who Stole my Hat?	Message in a Bottle	Flying with Bears
The Deathless Ones	One More Day	Two out of Ten
Bride of Fire	The Doom Groom	Nettle Tea
Dream Stealers	Lost Faces	Three Years Later

Variation:

You can also take the titles of songs, or even lyrics, and develop loglines from those.

WHAT'S GOING ON?

Your task:

For this solo exercise you need an image containing people, or something you can characterise, whether it be a robot, creature, or flowerpot. You can pretty much characterise anything.

It doesn't have to be the perfect image, just something where someone/something is in a location, so not a random portrait of someone's head. There can be multiple people, but you will still centre everything on one of them.

Avoid using an image of someone you know, as you want it to be without any immediate personal meaning.

If you're stuck with where to find an image, try image libraries, going to a gallery, or search online. You can also look on news sites, but if you do that, be prepared to read about lots of misery.

Once you have that image, write:

1. What is going on in the image.
2. What happened just before the image was taken.
3. What is going to happen next.

You should end up writing around a paragraph for each point.

Why this helps?
Whether you're writing a script or a book, it's visual, in that images are being created or presented.

You'll find that having an image in front of you with a character in a setting allows you to develop them more fully, make them more rounded, and feel more alive. It also triggers so much more than staring at a blank page.

Because stories have a beginning, middle, and end, and the events that link everything together, you'll find that thinking about what has happened before and after your image will shape a story.

In the past, writing students have found that this also helps them to think of other characters that link to the story and a theme starts to emerge.

It's also pressure free, because this doesn't have to be in any story you're writing, but often, when looking for a new idea, this forms the basis for a set of important, narratively linked moments.

NEWSWORTHY

This solo exercise is about engaging with what's going on in the world to find inspiration.

A news story gave me my writing break. I had a sitcom optioned, which means a company paid to have the exclusive right to pitch my comedy to broadcasters for a set time. Sadly, nothing came of it. However, we liked working together, so they suggested I pitch for an anthology series about celebrity stories that they were working on.

I did my research, and found a story about when Muhammad Ali saved someone from jumping from a building in the 1980s. With a co-writer, we turned that into a twenty-two-minute episode that was part of a season nominated for an International Emmy for best drama. We lost to *Money Heist*, which is fair enough.

So, sometimes researching and news stories can highlight drama you can expand on. We had a lot to do to dramatise the story and to make it sustain the time slot, but a lot of what we needed was done for us by its existence. We had the character, the central drama, and the setting.

Allow yourself to find inspiration in the world around you.

Small stories often have big themes, so take the time to think about them. It can be truly rewarding.

Your task:

1. Spend twenty minutes searching for news stories. Note the ones you find interesting.
    - Use the full twenty minutes, as even if you find something great, there could be something else inspiring.
2. Once the twenty minutes ends, look at your list. Which is the most interesting story to you and why?
3. Whatever you select, consider why the person in the story did what they did.
4. Write what happened before and after this story took place.
5. Now write a logline for it.

Research tip: If you're unsure of where to start looking, you can:

- Look at news websites or newspapers, but avoid the main stories.
- Search for lists. For example: "Facts about..." and you'll find interesting angles on topics.
- Read magazines to do with a certain topic.
- Look up regional/state specific news, as those focus more on people than miserable global events.

For the Muhammad Ali story, I searched a lot of things before I found it, including:

- Weird celebrity stories.
- Interesting celebrity facts.

- Celebrity once injured by…
- Amazing things famous people have done.

There was a lot more which had varying results until I found the story.

Why this helps?

Its main purpose is to have you connect character to drama.

By deciding why you think the person in the story did what they did, you'll better understand motivated actions.

Also, in understanding why you're interested in the story, it may unearth more about your voice.

News stories are drama. They are also written in a way that gets to the point, so it's a good way to understand economy of storytelling. Plus, you'll gain valuable research skills which is essential to any writer.

Coming up with something from nothing is also incredibly difficult, and if you're feeling sluggish or empty of ideas, finding existing stories is a great way to ignite your creativity.

GENRE SHIFT

This solo or group exercise is about reimagining.

Your task:
Take a story you know well. It can be a fairytale, a film, anything. Now flip the genre and write a description of it.

For example, what if *Ted Lasso* was really a detective story about an undercover agent sent in as an unqualified coach to investigate fraud at a football club?

You might even decide that *Schitt's Creek* is a horror where a rich family loses everything and has to live in a motel, but the inhabitants of the town all want to kill the family.

Go wild, and continue developing the idea out, thinking of the characters and the key moments in the story.

Why this helps?
It allows you the freedom to take existing characters and flip

their characteristics into different contexts. It will help you to understand genre further, and you might surprise yourself with how you can create an interesting character in a genre where some archetypes feel overused.

OUT OF THIN AIR

It's hard to pluck an idea out of thin air. Or is it? In this solo exercise we're going to try.

Your task:

1. Look around. The next person you see is your character. If you're at home, maybe look out of the window.
2. Write down ten things about them from personality traits to favourite biscuit. Anything.
3. Look around where you are and pick a colour. What emotion does that represent? That's how your character feels today.
4. Why do they feel that way?
5. Whatever the next thing you smell is, that triggers a memory for your character. What is that memory?
6. Listen. What is the first sound you hear?
7. Build a scene where that sound is the centre of a situation. For example, a dripping might inspire you

    to place your character in a leaky loft during a storm, trying to figure out what to do.
8. What is the story this scene is a small part of?

Why this helps?

By immersing ourselves in our surroundings, we can create anything. And by focusing that immersion and getting narrower with each step, we might discover a story.

I WANT

Do this exercise alone and be honest with yourself to get the most out of it.

Your task:
Write down:

1. Twenty things you want. Anything from a sandwich to something bigger in your life.
2. Why you want each thing and how it will make you feel to have it.
3. What is stopping you from getting the thing you want.

Why this helps?
By reflecting on a list of small and big wants, you'll see how you can make drama out of anything.

You'll also get a stronger handle on what drama is. It's

someone wanting something but it not coming so easily. From your list you'll realise some things wouldn't sustain a minute, while others need to be unpacked further.

Through reflecting on your own motivations and flaws, you'll have a stronger grasp of character.

THE WORST IDEAS

This task is better done with others, but still works if you want to do it alone. The focus is on not being ashamed to share bad or poorly formed ideas.

Your task (if alone):

- Spend ten minutes writing down bad ideas.
- Once finished, choose one and spend ten minutes expanding on the world, characters, and story.

Your task (with others):

- Each person takes turns pitching a bad idea.
- After each pitch, the other writers ask questions to see if you can expand the world, characters, and story.

Why this helps?

Bad ideas are part of the process, and this will help you to embrace the imperfection of development and idea generation.

If you're a screenwriter and you're ever in a writing room, bad ideas are welcome, as someone might see an angle that elevates it.

This will also help you to analyse why an idea might be bad, so you can understand what makes a good idea.

Through questioning the idea, you might also find some good in it and realise that nothing is unsalvageable.

TIPS

Rather than calling it the first draft or the charmingly named vomit draft, think of it as a discovery draft, where you're feeling things out. Nobody else needs to see it.

Write what you care about and write what you would enjoy. If you're not enjoying writing, then stop and think why.

Writing is a process of imperfection, so don't be precious. Rewriting is your friend.

You can write at the computer, but it's hard to create while staring at a screen. Inspiration comes when you engage with the world and move.

Respect writing and make it part of your daily routine.

Originality is in your observations and what you want to say about something.

Trying to create is hard. Go easy on yourself. Results come from kindness, not self-loathing.

The worst idea is the one you don't explore.

Don't fear rejection. It's part of the process. Go and get your first and start your journey.

Writing is like exercise. The more you do it, the sooner you see results and the better you feel.

You will always make mistakes. The journey is learning from them.

Do the dishes. Hoover. Go for a walk. Let your subconscious get to work.

CHARACTER AND MOTIVATION

Character is the heart and soul of our story. I won't ramble too long, as I've written a book on it called: *The Craft of Character*.

But whatever you're doing, always remind yourself that stories are about people with problems to overcome. External and internal.

Some exercises in this section are from the book I've just mentioned, but I've created plenty of new ones.

Most are about your protagonist, so when I use the word "character" I really mean protagonist unless otherwise specified.

OPPOSITES

This solo or group exercise looks at how drama comes from character and their internal and external conflict. We're going to create contradictions.

Your task:

Take a certain type of character and think of what a contradiction would be, or what might not belong together. For example: a priest who writes erotic novels.

That's a start. Then we need to get into why? Maybe it's to save his church from ruin and his novels make good money.

This gives me plenty of oppositional forces, and I begin to think of things from character, such as how and why he got into writing erotic novels and who else is in his life. What even made erotic novels seem like an option to him? Does he have a parent in this industry? Did that make him turn to religion? This is all top-of-the-head thinking, but we're getting somewhere and with each potential answer more questions emerge that lead to a deeper exploration.

It also makes me think of the place, as a small town would be more intimate and riskier than a city, with some of the locals probably reading the priest's erotic novels.

So:

1. Think of a person.
2. What is at odds with who they are?
3. Why are they doing what they do?

If you need inspiration:

Here's a table with some people and contradictions.

The interesting thing in all of these will be the "Why?". That's where observations, deeper characterisation, motivation, and our unique voice come through.

Who	Contradiction
Detective	Steals from his daughter's school
Ex-wrestler with anger issues	Has to look after his estranged niece
An escaped murderer	Finds an abandoned baby
A grieving recluse	Finds a sick hedgehog
A young ICE agent	Has to arrest his former nanny
A homeless person	Wins the lottery
A teenager	Witnesses their parent murder someone

Why this helps?

You'll create stronger internal and external conflict, allowing you to see the complications that can emerge through the character trying to achieve what they want.

You'll also create from character. Through the questions that emerge you'll unpack a life, and the character will feel like a person with history, relationships, experiences, and views. It will all come from within.

The "Why?" will also help you to remember the importance of motive and making something plausible.

CHARACTER FROM A LOGLINE

This solo exercise is my favourite from my book *The Craft of Character*, as it makes you think about character in connection to the story, and it encourages structure to emerge from your protagonist.

The logline contains the key elements of story: the protagonist, the antagonistic force, the inciting incident, and the action, which also suggests stakes. I expand on loglines in the earlier intro for the part: *Creating Ideas*

The logline is our guide whenever we get lost in the writing, but it's also a rich area to pull character from, which leads to more authentic storytelling. Many of us have a habit of throwing plot at character, rather than delving into their lives to find it.

Your task:

Take your logline, for example:

When a cynical 35-year-old woman has a heart attack, she has to change the way she approaches life, or she won't make it to forty.

Then highlight the key words. I generally do this on paper, circling words connected to character and story. You can just bold them if you prefer to use a computer. So:

*When a **cynical** 35-year-old woman **has a heart attack**, she **has to change** the way she approaches life, or she **won't make it to forty**.*

Then, look at those bolded words and ask "Why?" multiple times.

Why is she cynical? Why did she have a heart attack? What in her life contributed to that? Relationships? Work? Health? Was it self-destruction? Does she need therapy? Is there one event that caused it or multiple events?

Then I'll do the same for her having to change. How much does she want to change? There's conflict there.

From this, different ideas, all connected to my protagonist will emerge, such as relationships, where she lives etc... When it comes to someone being stressed, do I get more out of her living in a city she's just moved to, or the quiet countryside where she grew up? What questions about her form from each choice?

Have fun with it and keep asking "Why?" like an excited toddler, eager to understand the world. In excitement and curiosity, creativity can run wild.

Why this helps?

It will pull story from character rather than you just throwing arbitrary plots at them. It also creates layers, and things like cynicism in my example will be more deeply connected rather than just a loose characteristic. Your protagonist's reasons for doing things will be more truthful, and their history will emerge.

As you interrogate the key details of your logline, you'll naturally think of story, your character in relation to other characters, and their world. Everything will begin to feel more unique.

We are creating lives when we put characters on the page. Those lives have been lived up to the point we join them and have experiences, traumas, and emotions to generate conflict from.

BUILD A LIFE

This solo exercise is about observing to create.

Your task:

Go to a public place if you are able to. Somewhere like a cafe or library, and observe someone in a non-creepy way. Please. Nobody needs a creep in their day. Don't stare. Don't point. Don't grunt at random people.

Then, write answers to the following questions:

1. What is their name, age, and occupation?
2. Why are they here?
3. What kind of home do they live in?
4. Who is their best friend and why?
5. What is their biggest regret in life?
6. What do they want more than anything?
7. What is stopping them achieving their goal?
8. What is their greatest fear?
9. What is a secret they've never told anyone?

Tip: Don't go with the very first thought that comes to mind, as it'll often be the most stereotypical or familiar.

Why this helps?

By focusing on one person, it'll improve your concentration skills. You'll also consider the first thoughts you have about someone based on their appearance.

It'll also give you a platform to create from. The way someone sits, what they've ordered, who they're with, and their body language, will all trigger thoughts. We can attribute intention and character to everything if we try.

WHAT WOULD YOU DO?

This solo exercise is about understanding what your character would do in any given situation.

Your task:

Take a character from a story you're already writing, or create an entirely new one. Then write down what they would do in five of the following scenarios, and why they would make that choice. You're welcome to do more.

If you're feeling inspired, you could even write out the scenes. What would they do if:

- They witness their mother stealing from a shop?
- They see an old man being bullied on the bus?
- They realise a colleague they're in love with has plagiarised their work?
- They see their mentor cheating on their partner?
- They're offered everything they ever wanted if they betray their best friend?
- They discover a wallet full of cash including an ID?

- They run into their ex after three years of not speaking?
- They find an old love/hate letter they never sent?
- They switch bodies with someone they don't like or respect?
- They're running late for an important meeting, and find an injured fox on the side of the street?

Now for a twist... Write down what YOU would do in three of the scenarios and why?

Why this helps?

Often, our actions are indicators of our intentions, so by placing people in dramatic scenarios, you get to see their true values.

By doing the exercise on yourself, you'll also tap into psychology. Creating characters has an element of therapy to it, so understanding the "Why?" is crucial to improving your character creation skills.

Also, it's a low-pressure way to get your character interacting with the world in random scenes, which may also inspire the creation of secondary characters, or issues in their life that need resolving.

What this could look like:

I'm inspired by the scenario: *They're running late for an important meeting, and find an injured fox on the side of the street.*

I think about a person, perhaps a middle-aged woman who is the sole-earner in her marriage, who recently lost her father to a hit-and-run accident. Normally, she might leave that wounded animal and think about it later and whether she should have stopped, but because of what happened to her father, she takes the fox to a local veterinary practice.

When she arrives at the office she explains the situation to her boss, but he's not interested as he needed her at the meeting with investors. He fires her and puts her on gardening leave.

She doesn't tell her husband, as there's a lot of pressure on their finances. Instead, she pretends she's still going to work each morning, but goes to volunteer at the veterinary practice, where through caring for the fox and other animals she reconnects with herself, confronts the guilt about her relationship with her father, and finds the courage to leave her dying marriage.

From one prompt I've got a story about grief, a character, secondary characters, complications in her life, and a journey of rediscovery. Maybe she only worked that job to help her husband (a childhood sweetheart), who doesn't treat her well. More questions all tied to character emerge.

From a death she will rediscover life.

LETTER FROM YOUR PROTAGONIST

This solo exercise is about embodying your character. It's worth having a vague sense of what your story is about to make this exercise worthwhile.

Your task:

Write a letter/email/voice note/ text exchange from your protagonist to you.

It can be as long as you want, but ideally no less than a page. Their goal is to convince you to write their story, or depending on who they are, maybe they want to convince you of the opposite.

They are addressing you directly, and you could consider the following questions in their communication:

- Why do they think their story needs to be told or not told?
- How do they approach this communication?
- How do they view themselves?
- What would they say to get what they want in this exchange?

- What aspects of their story do they think are worth sharing?

Why this helps?

This exercise places you in your character's mind and helps you to capture their voice, their beliefs, their motivation, and the emotion. It also highlights what you, the writer, find interesting about the character journey. That's something you often need to remind yourself of as you're taking notes and rewriting.

Through writing as your protagonist you might reveal interesting story points you'll want to include in the narrative. For example, my character may tell me I need to tell their story because they nearly murder someone. That could end up being in the story I write.

What this could look like:

Let's imagine I have a TV comedy series about an ambitious young woman who is stuck reporting on local news stories, but wants to report on national news and big, worthy items. I'm imagining these are voice notes:

> Mark,
>
> I hope you're well (I have to say that or I appear rude, right?). Sorry, just having a coffee while I send these, waiting for my camera op, Patty, to turn up. She had a big night, again...
>
> Anyway, you need to write about my life. Honestly. It's funny, mostly because it's tragic, but I'm hoping there's a happy ending.

I work in online news in East Anglia, not because I want to, but because of my family name. You see, my dad is a national treasure, much loved journalist Harry Deagle, and you'd think he'd open some doors, but no, this is some sort of reverse nepotism where he's got me a terrible job working for a woman he's sleeping with who likes to control me to keep him close. There are good stories here, but she gives me the rubbish ones that get about four views. I've had to report on a man who made the world's biggest flag, the hundred-year anniversary of a bench, two sharks being married at an aquarium, and I'm about to report on Banham Zoo getting a penguin. Yep. That's news, and they're having a launch on Friday…

My girlfriend is currently working at the BBC reporting on real issues. I just can't seem to catch a break.

So, me and Patty have decided to make the stories dramatic. It was mostly her idea, but as she's endlessly drunk - she's reeling from a divorce - it's on me to make it work. We're going to sneak into the zoo, borrow the penguin… Hear me out. Borrow the penguin and treat it wonderfully. Patty has a big bath it can stay in and I'll buy it some fish. Then we'll wait for the fallout and the story to break. Then on the morning of the event we'll 'find' the penguin, and conveniently be the first to report its return. It'll generate publicity for the launch event and get more eyes on the story. It's genius. From four viewers to viral, and hopefully I'll get spotted by a bigger channel.

So, yeah, I doubt anything will go wrong. It's a pretty solid plan and Patty's flatmate can keep guard when we're out. I'll have to keep it a secret from my girlfriend as she won't approve. Maybe I'll tell her one day.

> So write about my life. I'm ambitious, and I will make the national news. I just want to be able to escape my boss, step out of my dad's shadow, and show my girlfriend I'm worthy. Weirdly, when I first met Patty I thought she was a lunatic, but she's just wounded and the most fun I have right now is trying to make stories more interesting with her. I will grow my profile and I will make a difference. Don't miss out.

It's messy and scattered, but I'm getting a sense of her voice, her stubbornness, her inferiority complex masked by ambition, and the lengths she'll go to in order to prove herself. I'm seeing many flaws, and some good beats of a story. The idea that she wants to build a profile is fun. For example, I'll give her national exposure, but as part of a scandal for stealing the penguin. It's a comedy, so I want to give her hope then humiliate her on a large scale. Her goal is to go viral, so I'll give her what she wants in the worst way possible.

This is emerging to me as a story about self-worth, as reflected in some of the relationships she's mentioned.

SECONDARY CHARACTERS

This solo or group exercise is about how secondary characters should feel connected to the story, but also be distinct from your protagonist.

Your task:

Take three or more characters who are not your protagonist, then place them in one of the heightened situations coming up and write the scene, paying particular attention to how they would each act.

It's up to you to add anything you want. For example, in the second prompt where they run over a deer, the driver could be drunk, or the car might be borrowed. It's up to you to raise the tension and drama of the situation using your own creativity. Don't hold back.

Here are some suggested situations, but do feel free to come up with your own:

- They get stuck in a lift.
- They run over a deer in the middle of the night.
- They catch a friend's lover cheating.

- There's a fight between two people they know.
- They're asked to lie for your protagonist (who is not in the scene).
- They're at a funeral and all feel differently about the deceased.
- They see a robbery taking place.
- On a hike, one of them gets seriously injured while a storm is coming.
- They're on a holiday and have woken up to find their belongings stolen.

Why this helps?

This helps you to identify the differences between your characters to prevent them sounding similar. When I say characters sound the same, I don't mean purely in how they speak, but in what they value, their wants, fears, and worldviews.

People often reveal themselves in a crisis and under pressure, so it will help you to understand your characters better.

It's about the external stressors bringing out the internal issues. This will get you writing dialogue and action to capture voice and belief.

QUOTES

We're used to reading quotes from people in the news and hearing soundbites from interviews. From these snippets, we often label people. This solo exercise is all about building from those labels.

Your task:

Find a quote. It can be from history, from a musician, anyone, anywhere.

Then disregard the person who said it, and create a new character from that quote. Write answers to the following questions:

- Why did they say what they said?
- How do they feel about the world?
- What do they want to achieve by saying what they said?
- What belief is behind what they have said?
- What are they afraid of?
- What good thing could happen because of what they said?

- What bad thing could happen because of what they said?

Why this helps?

By building from a quote, you already have a strong standpoint from a character, as it's them expressing something. By taking that and digging into the why behind it, you'll find depths that inform motivation, experience, and fear.

People are rounded, and we don't just say things for the sake of it. Behind any statement is a belief and an intention, and hope for a particular outcome.

REPRESENT

This solo task is about understanding how characters contribute to your core message, which is what the story is really about.

This exercise works best if you already have a sense of your protagonist's arc. Some writers need to write a draft or two to discover the message, so don't feel like you've done something wrong if that's you. We all have different processes and I'm one of those writers. It's fine to have a vague idea at the start.

Your task:

1. Write your story's core message in the middle of a page.
   - For example, I may have a character in a dying marriage who is doing everything out of fear, and by the end, after everything they've been through, makes a choice out of love. So, the message is: "Love will set you free."
   - If you're unsure of your message, focus on your protagonist's journey. In what way are they

changing? What do they believe at the beginning that changes by the end?
2. Write what your protagonist represents in relation to the message at the start. How do they embody the opposite of the message? In my case, my character wants to stay in a toxic marriage, which comes from fear. They believe they can make their partner fall in love with them again, instead of facing the truth.
3. Brainstorm different ideas that represent alternatives to your character.
    - For example, if my character is in a toxic marriage and wants to stay there, they likely have a weak sense of self, so perhaps I'll write: someone who is unashamedly themselves. A happy marriage. Someone desperate for love etc...
4. Create characters from your ideas.
    - From the ideas some will feel like characters to develop. A happy marriage could be shown in a neighbour, so he can see what a real home looks like. Maybe there's someone he finds annoying who he eventually sees as someone who doesn't hide and throws love into everything, risking hurt. Perhaps the partner he wants back is someone who truly embodies fear and control.

The characters will embody these behaviours so that the protagonist can see different ways of being in action. If you have a story about grief, what does each character represent about grief and what are they all grieving? How do they all cope with their grief?

Why this helps?
The characters around your protagonist should reflect, chal-

lenge, or blur the core message or question at the heart of the story. This helps to deepen your theme and bring out internal conflict through the external relationship dynamics.

It will connect everything, making for a more coherent experience, and your characters will all earn their place in the story.

PEACE TALKS

Your task:
In this solo exercise, you'll write a scene where you place your protagonist and villain/antagonist in a setting of your choosing. Here, they will have clear-the-air talks. Write freely, but if you want ideas, you can consider:

- How do they justify their behaviour?
- How do they try to make the other person see their point of view?
- What do they hope to achieve by clearing the air?
- How do they feel about the person opposite them and why?

If you find the peace talks collapse and there's a huge fallout, follow it. Start with the intention of peace, and see where creativity takes you.

Why this helps?
This exercise will help you to further understand motivation in your protagonist and antagonist/villain. Every character is

motivated and wants something in the story, and the worst thing you can do is write a surface-level antagonist/villain. It's worth remembering Christopher Vogler's words in *The Writer's Journey*: "Every villain is a hero of his or her own story."

You'll also expand on your narrative from character, as inevitably the characters will discuss moments that could or could not be part of the spine of your story.

FIRST IMPRESSIONS

This solo exercise embraces the idea that first impressions matter. From the moment we meet a character, we're creating a profile.

Often, the best way to introduce someone is in an action to do with who they are and the type of story we're about to experience.

For example, in *Whiplash* we meet Andrew Neiman drumming, then Fletcher enters and exerts his dominance. It shows how Andrew is desperate to be a drummer, and how hard Fletcher is on people, and also communicates the psychological tone and status dynamics that will continue through the film.

In an action film we're likely to meet the hero immediately in a dangerous situation to set up who they are and how good they are at what they do, so do pay attention to genre.

Your task:
Look at the list of occupations, or come up with your own:

- Therapist
- Teacher

- Cleaner
- Nanny
- Swimmer
- Tree surgeon
- Hypnotist
- Assassin
- Bank manager
- Plumber

Choose one. Add a characteristic to the person, pick a genre, and then write an introductory scene that communicates who the person is, what they want, and delivers on tone.

Why this helps?

The way you introduce your protagonist creates expectation, intrigue, and places tone. The opening is one of the hardest things to get right in a story, but can have multiple layers if you really think about your protagonist and their journey.

HUMANISE IT

This solo exercise is all about perspective and physically holding something.

Your task:

Find an object in your home. It can be anything from a handbag to an urn.

- Hold it.
- Think about where it started life.
- Where was it before it came into your life?
- What was the most interesting thing it ever saw in your home or while with you?
- What was the most interesting thing it saw before you possessed it?
- What is the worst thing it has ever seen?
- What six key events has the object been around for in your life?

Why this helps?

By characterising even the blandest of objects, you'll get a sense of drama. In humanising an object you'll also have fun drawing upon its characteristics that you can express. For example, if I humanise a desk, it may be grumpy because of people who have scratched their names into its wood. It may have started life in a small office, but was sold when its owner had to close their business, so has attachment issues.

FLIP IT

This solo or group exercise is about how a simple change can have profound results.

Your task:

Take a character from your story or a well-known one from a story you know.

- Flip the gender, or if you want, make them an animal.
- How do they see the world differently?
- What about them has changed?

Why this helps?

Sometimes you can see an entirely new story by flipping the gender. Years ago I wrote a script about someone who inherited a restaurant they didn't want, and I wrote my protagonist as a female version of Larry David. Producers loved it. It got optioned, never got made, but got me more work because it felt fresh at a time when female roles were only used to prop up the male leads.

BAD TO THE BONE

This solo task is for those of you who are too protective of your main character and scared to let them make bad decisions.

Your task:

- List ten of the worst things your protagonist has ever done in their lives and why.
    - They can be from before, during, and after the timeline of your story.
- Write out one of those moments as a scene.

Why this helps?

We can be too overprotective of our protagonist and leave the drama to those around them. In those cases the story ends up happening to your protagonist rather than them happening to the story. It leads to inactivity.

By writing a scene of them being bad that isn't in your story, you'll see that their action is motivated, and that connection isn't in likability, but in understanding. If we can understand why someone does what they do, even if it's bad, it creates a chance for connection.

What this could look like:

From a list I write, I may be intrigued by: *They once saw a jilted bride in a supermarket two days after she had been left at the altar, and asked for their honeymoon contribution back to buy concert tickets.*

That's not horrible, as to be fair, the couple didn't get married, so my character should get their money back. But it's not considerate of the jilted bride's feelings and the timing is awful. However, my character needs those tickets before they sell out, so in their mind, they are justified in their actions.

It is bad on my character's part in terms of social etiquette and empathy, but I can have fun with it. I can think about how they know the bride and groom. Do they even like them? Is it one of those weddings people go to not really wanting to? Will they end up taking the bride to the concert?

Then I would write the scene.

ARGUE WITH YOURSELF

Your task:
This solo exercise is about a healthy debate with yourself.

1. Take a strong belief you have. It could be that capitalism is awful, dogs are better than cats, or that if you want something done properly you need to do it yourself.
2. Write down why you believe this.
3. Now write down all the reasons why your belief could be wrong. You might research articles or arguments for the alternative belief.

Why this helps?

Characters in stories often have strong beliefs that hinder internal transformation. By tapping into your own you'll better understand how deep motivation goes and what moment(s) consolidated your belief.

By arguing the counterpoint you'll gain a better understanding of alternative views, and you'll see how far you go to protect your belief. This helps you to create characters with stronger conviction.

TIPS

Don't protect your main character. Let them make bad decisions.

Character is everything.

Understanding character is about understanding humanity.

If you can't answer the question "Why?", stop. Think. "Why?" is the fuel in this engine.

Much like characters in a story, the writer's journey is full of highs and lows.

We don't remember moments in stories, we remember who those moments happen to, or because of.

If you're stuck, go back to character. Why are they doing what they're doing?

Treat yourself to nice notebooks, but never show anyone what's inside them.

If you find your characters taking over the writing, listen.

STORY WORLD

Something I often see ignored in early writing is the world of the story. I've read plenty of stories, from road movies where the journey is generic and nondescript, to workplace sitcoms where the workplace isn't understood beyond the surface and could've been written by anyone.

The world of your story is incredibly important. It's not only the space in which your story operates, but also:

- The time.
- The values people live by.
- The specific areas of conflict and interaction.
- The established systems.
- The habitual events.
- The rules.
- The history.
- The choices that have already been made. It's not day one, unless it actually is.

Wherever you're setting your story, do your research, make it feel authentic, and you'll see the benefits in how it connects to your character's journey. Specificity also leads to a more memorable experience for your audience.

The following exercises will help you to better realise the world your characters exist in.

WHAT HAPPENED HERE?

Your task:
In this solo exercise, you'll choose two locations from your story world. They can be a public or private space, even one in the character's home.

Answer the following questions:

- What is its history?
- Is it a place of meaning to your character? If so, why?
- What is the best memory they have had here or will have here during the story?
- What is the worst memory they have had here or will have here?
- How did they feel the first time they entered?
- What does your character do in this place?
- Who is an important character that is often in this space? And what is their relationship to your protagonist?
- How does the space link to your protagonist's personality?

Why this helps?

This will help you to tie your character to place, and to understand how they interact with the world around them.

If they are someone who regularly goes to dive bars or glamorous ones, we'll want to understand why as it will say something about them and how they feel in those spaces.

In the TV show, *Friends,* Central Perk was an important meeting point where the main characters frequently had coffee. It would've been odd to have the group spend time there, but never interact with secondary characters. That's why Gunther, the manager, knew them and had moments with them.

The strength of the location also allowed the writers to come up with a storyline in which outside characters sat on the sofa where the main characters always sat, which created a crisis for two of them.

Locations are reflections of people and are rich areas for story and conflict.

WHAT DO I SEE?

Your task:
In this solo task, you'll try to see through your protagonist's eyes.

Your protagonist is going to look outside of their window and write down what they see, in their voice.

If you're writing a character who can't see, then perhaps imagine them outside and moving so you can feel how they would explore the world around them.

If you don't yet have a character, do this as yourself and really think about what you see and how it makes you feel.

If it helps, think about:

- What time of day it is.
- What they can see directly ahead.
- What the weather is like.
- What they can see at the end of their street.
- What kind of people they might see.
- How they feel about this view, their home, their street, the people etc...

Why this helps?

This will place you, as your protagonist, in the world of the story. You'll start to understand how they feel about the world, their place within it, and the people around them. Sometimes we don't live where we want, or in a situation we're happy with. Other times, we may look outside of our window with extreme pride at what we've achieved.

Get into the mind of your protagonist, as understanding their sense of self in connection to place allows for greater depth and authenticity.

ADVENTURE TIME

This one is a little trickier and may not apply to everyone. It should be done solo to get the most out of it.

If you cannot go to the place your story is set, then consider somewhere that may be similar. For example, if you set your story in an Italian village but live in the UK, then find a village that may share some characteristics with the Italian one.

Of course, if you're writing something historical, or something set in a maximum-security prison, then you'll be limited in what you can do. That's where it's important to make even more effort in your research.

Your task:

You can do this two ways:

1. If you have a story and character you're working on, become your character (you don't need to dress up). Walk around the area you've set your story, or its equivalent.

2. If you don't have an existing character, choose somewhere and walk around to really observe and feel what it's like as yourself.

While exploring, pay attention to the sights, smells, sounds, the people who walk around. Feel the energy. Places have characteristics and a feeling.

Why this helps?
Specificity creates authenticity, and you might think of ways to bring your character into conflict with some of the unique parts of a particular world.

I once wrote a film set somewhere I had never been to. Did I go there to do my research? No. I was lazy and also broke. Instead, I used Google Earth and read a lot around the location. It meant my script was pretty specific, and I was commended for it, but there was more I could've done.

A decade later, I visited the place on holiday with my wife, and the live experience gave me so much more. I noticed how seagulls shrieked from morning until night. I saw how the tide receded to the point you could walk the entire coast for a few hours. I observed how busy it was during school holidays, especially with narrow pavements. There was a long list of experiences that showed me I could write something more authentic and connect my character's issues to the environmental stressors and unique characteristics of the setting.

If you can, get out there and live it like your characters would.

IF IT WAS A PERSON

Bear with me, this solo task is weird, but fun. If you've been writing long enough, you've probably heard someone say that the setting is a character. That is absolutely true, and this exercise embraces that idea.

Your task:
Take a location from your day-to-day life, or your story if you're in the middle of one or developing it.

1. Spend ten minutes writing a list of all the things you can think of about the place. Get as detailed as you want.
2. Then characterise it. As in, if it was a person, what would they be like?

Describe the person. For example, a miserable pub stuck in the 80s may get you thinking about someone with a mullet who tells the same stories over and over, and hasn't come to terms with their divorce, hence they're stuck in the past (sorry mullet people. I love mullets and wish I could grow one).

Go deeper than that, but you can see how a location characteristic can be linked to a human one based on your own perceptions, biases, and experiences. Lean into it and have fun.

If you're unsure, think about these:

- What does the human version (or animal, robot etc...) look like?
- What do they value?
- How do they interact with the world?
- What do they want from life?
- How do they feel about themselves and why?

Why this helps?

This helps you to think beyond the obvious and to characterise your location on multiple levels. It may unlock some interesting symbolism too. With this exercise, you should be able to better visualise, and therefore describe the place.

It makes you observe, consider, and in a lot of cases, appreciate things you otherwise might ignore.

It also shows you how places can reflect things about characters in your story.

SOUNDTRACK TO THE SCENE

This solo exercise embraces how every place has a unique atmosphere, from the visuals and energy to the sound.

Your task:

- Think of a setting from your story or make one up. It could be anywhere: a beach, an alien spacecraft, a hotel, or an emergency room.
- Write down five distinct sounds in that setting, and be specific.
    - For example, rather than writing "children", it could be a child shouting that they found a seashell.
    - Think of distance. What sounds are close or far away?
- Now write a paragraph about how your character hears these things and how they make them think or feel.
    - Does something connect to a memory?

- Does something bring them joy or discomfort?

If you have a character with hearing difficulties, how do they hear or feel the world differently?

Why this helps?
Senses contribute to the experience, and sound builds immersion. Sounds can also make a character feel safe or in danger, and are triggers for memories.

TIPS

That break-up scene you just wrote in a domestic setting; write it in a public place.

A good fantasy or sci-fi taps into what it is to be human. The rest is dressing.

Experience the world. The more you experience, the more you have to say, and the more you understand people.

Do your research. It doesn't mean you can't be creative. It means you're making creative choices from a place of information rather than ignorance.

Writing is about exploration.

Don't limit your thinking. Step outside of your comfort zone.

A lot of who we are is based on where we grew up. Places have a role in forming the person.

Every new story we write makes our world that little bit bigger.

STRUCTURE

Stories have a shape to them, and there are thousands of books on structure, so I'm not going to get into it, other than to remind you that structure is important, of course it is, but, if you impose structure on something too soon, you will destroy creative thinking and have a very well-functioning story that is bland.

So, know structure, use it well, but don't obsess about it. Structure is only great when it comes from character and helps you to see ways to make their story more dramatic. Character is structure. Structure grows out of them, what they're trying to do, and our understanding of them.

The following exercises are designed to remind you of that.

BEGINNING, MIDDLE, AND END

This solo or group exercise focuses on the importance of visualisation in storytelling, whatever the form. If we're not being presented with images, we're imagining them from the words on the page.

The way people interpret our descriptions is up to them, but we can be deliberate in what we're trying to do. Our job is to build the roads. It's up to people how they walk down them, if they walk down them at all.

Your task:

1. Find an image. Any one image that resonates with you.
2. Decide whether it's the beginning, middle, or end of a story.
3. Then imagine what the other two images are, writing out their descriptions.

You don't have to draw. Write what you're seeing in each

image to create cohesion. If you enjoy drawing, then go for it, or even use an AI image generator and see how it interprets what you describe.

Variation:
If you're stuck on an existing story, take an image from a key point and apply the exercise.

Why this helps?
If you're stuck with structure, sometimes you need to go back to the imagery to understand emotion and how things link. Aristotle argued that stories are a chain of cause-and-effect actions, with each action inspiring the next until the story reaches its end.

This exercise will help you to visualise, and then attach meaning to images that imply the emotional state of a character at pivotal story points. Then you can build the other moments from emotions that are tied to character.

Images carry symbolism, meaning, and subtext. All of those are attached to character.

This will also help you to see whether your ending should actually be your midpoint.

What this could look like:
I may be curious about an image I find of a middle-aged man throwing a briefcase into the sea.

It could represent a lot of different things. Someone throwing away some evidence. A man having a breakdown. Someone who has just been fired. I let my mind run with it.

I might decide that it is the end of the story. Perhaps it represents him freeing himself from society and the grind. Then I consider who he is at the start, and who he is at the midpoint, and describe what those images look like and what they represent.

So, at the start, he could be a struggling family man who ties his self-worth to what he can provide, and he makes a deal with a corrupt businessman. That image could be:

He's at home in the living room, sat on a broken sofa, looking at a business card in his hand. He looks exhausted and is dressed in worn out clothes. Behind him, his wife feeds their young crying son at a makeshift table made of boxes while looking over at him, but he's not engaging. The wall needs painting, there's a broken window covered by a plank of wood, and a flickering light bulb.

This suggests that while he wants to fix things, he's not present in what is important. The environment around him is symbolic of his internal struggle.

Then in the middle his deal works out, but in his pursuit of status and his growing ego, his family leaves him. That image could be:

In that same living room, he is in a suit, and the room has been painted, the window fixed, the light illuminating everything, and a new table in place of the boxes. Only, his wife and son aren't at that table. There's simply a note on it.

Through that, I have someone who believes in something at the beginning, that to have a happy family life he needs to provide at all costs. I can think about where that belief comes from. Did his parents divorce because of money troubles? Or at least, is that why he thinks they divorced? Suddenly I have a character with trauma, belief, and something to lose (his family), if he can't resolve his deeper issues. Perhaps on this journey he will reconcile with one of his parents or see them differently.

Layers begin to form. Things will change and improve, but now they exist.

Let images awaken your curiosity.

WHO DO I BECOME?

This solo exercise looks at your character's internal and external transformation.

Your task:
Take your protagonist and write down the following about them at the start of the story:

- What they do day to day.
- What they believe is the right way to live life.
- Where this belief comes from. Is it an experience that shaped them?
- What their priority is.
- Why their priority means so much.

Then, write down all the different versions of themselves they could be at the end of the story.

For example, if I have someone who at the start believes that avoiding interaction with the world is the right way to be, because interaction in the past led to hurt, then by the end they might be ready to interact again. They might be open to the gains and losses that come from being part of the world, as it's better for them and the relationships in their life. This is one interpretation.

Another could be that by the end, having tried to engage with the world, they see things as even more bleak, so double down and it's a tragedy. Or if it's a dark story, they kill the person they allowed to get close, sinking deeper into their decline.

The super happy version would be that they do something profound that shows the transition from individualism to community.

As you can see, it can go many ways, with varying degrees of joy or misery. Free your mind and have fun with it and lean into what you enjoy. Embrace what you feel a passion for.

Why this helps?

It forces you to write multiple ways in which something can end, which filters out the familiar or derivative, and gets you closer to your voice.

It helps you to remember that stories are about change, and by having your beginning and end, you can start to understand what your character needs to do to make that shift in mentality, whether it's a positive or negative one.

For me, writing without knowing your ending is like driving with no destination in mind and hoping for the best. Know your destination, then you can get there via multiple routes.

Things may change during the process, but by knowing where you're initially going, you have a sense of focused exploration, which ties in nicely with the next exercise.

IT STARTS WITH THE END

This solo exercise is about your story's emotional payoff.

Your task:
Write your ending. If you have a story, jump straight to the end and write the scene. If you're still in the development stages and are thinking about a character, write the end of their story anyway. If you've got nothing, go to the "Build a Life" exercise in the "Character and Motivation" section, do that, and then return.

Why this helps?
By beginning with the end, you know the emotional payoff, and you can chart the steps your character needs to take in order to arrive to this state.

The obstacles they encounter aren't just for fun, they have emotional meaning. They could highlight behaviours, actions, revelations that all in some way teach your character something, whether they're ready to receive that knowledge or not.

For example, if I have a character who starts the story selfish, but ends it selfless, then the obstacles along the way need to help with that change. Perhaps they see the positive impact of loyalty on the way, or are forced to be selfless to get out of trouble. Maybe they see the true consequences of selfishness.

Structure connects to the character's internal journey.

BREAK IT DOWN

This solo exercise focuses on the building blocks of story.

Most writers will have been advised at one stage to write their scenes on cards and stick them on the wall to keep track of everything. Being completely honest, that has never worked for me. I get bored half-way through and prefer to know key beats before writing, rather than every beat. It becomes too microscopic and mathematical for me.

It works wonderfully for some writers I know, so do what works for you and the way your brain operates.

What I found useful, was to take the idea of putting scenes on cards, but applying it to an existing piece of work.

Your task:

1. Choose a book/TV pilot/film/audio drama, ideally in the same genre you plan to write. It has to be something you can stop.
2. After every scene, pause.

3. Write a sentence highlighting the key dramatic event that occurs (some will be multi-beat scenes as storylines can intersect).
4. Describe the function of each scene. For example: set-up, inciting incident, break into two (the decision to act/enter the story), plan gone wrong, reveal of key information, midpoint etc... and how it ties to character.

Why this helps?

This exercise will help you to understand economy of storytelling, as some of these beats can occur in the same scene and don't all warrant an entire scene/chapter/or sequence.

This also helps you to see how stories keep pace and don't repeat emotional beats.

This taught me to bring my protagonist face to face with their goal at the midpoint, showing what success could look like for them, only to then make things harder, because they're not emotionally ready.

THE BLANK PAGE

This solo exercise is about you and the dreaded blank page.

To be honest, I love a blank page. It's full of opportunity and can be anything. For me, it represents hope.

What I dread is a page full of rubbish, which is the majority of first drafts I write and read. Even with my experience, every new first draft is a reminder of the long and beautifully imperfect process of writing.

However, the truth is, a page full of rubbish is something you can work with. A blank page is pure fantasy of what can be that you're not committing to. Jodi Picoult said:

"You can always edit a bad page, you can't edit a blank page."

With that in mind...

Your task:
Write a random scene between your protagonist and someone important from your story, but make sure it's a scene that isn't intended to be a part of your plot.

Put them into a setting and get them chatting without the constraints of structure and scene writing. Those things may naturally emerge during the process.

The scene can be as long as you like.

Why this helps?

It's pressure free. It's just you writing your characters, feeling them in the world and around each other.

I find when I use this exercise with writing students, most of the time the scene ends up being something the writer repurposes for the final script, as something organic emerges from the playfulness.

IMPROVE IT

Alone or in a group, it's time to enjoy a bad film.

We've all seen bad films. Some that are so bad we recommend them to our friends so that they can suffer too, and some that are so bad they somehow tip over into being entertaining.

However, it's easy to say something is bad. I will always appreciate anyone who has made something. It's such an exposing, brave thing to do. I think it's better to make something and be criticised than to sit around criticising. And often the issue with something considered bad, is that someone has gone ahead and made their first draft into the final product.

As a writer, my job when I see something bad now isn't to smugly call it awful and write something witty online to feel better about myself. It's to identify why it doesn't work, and then consider how I would make it better, which brings us onto the task.

Your task:
Find a bad film. It's subjective, and could be one you've seen,

or one you've always planned to watch. Some examples will follow. Then:

1. Watch a key bad scene.
2. Identify why it doesn't work.
3. Think of how you would make it better.
4. Rewrite it.

If you don't know of any, you can search for lists of bad films, otherwise here are some suggestions. Please do look up trigger warnings:

- *The Room.*
- *Troll 2.*
- *Hard Ticket to Hawaii.*
- *Birdemic: Shock and Terror.*

Why this helps?

It forces you to analyse and understand why something may not work. Rather than poke fun, you'll understand, and also develop some empathy.

You'll find you identify some shallow areas for improvement, then you'll start to look at character dynamics, genre, structure, and see that there are a lot of things that need to work together in order to create specific and engaging drama.

There are also things beyond the script that can make something bad, from the acting and directing to the music and editing. I worked on a show I won't name out of respect for everyone who poured love into it, where the rehearsals, actors, script, everything was wonderful, but when it was shot something simply didn't work. I think it was that the locations looked too gloomy, which didn't match the tone, but sometimes something simply doesn't come together.

WHOSE FAULT IS IT ANYWAY?

This solo or group exercise involves you looking at an existing story through a different lens. It's about humanising villains.

Your task:

Pick a story and write out moments from your villain's perspective.

For example, in *Jaws,* perhaps the shark attacked that swimmer because they were littering in the sea, and the film is really about climate change with the shark a tragic victim of humanity's destructive force.

That's just one moment, but take the main moments. If you need some beats, you can use these, but don't feel obliged to:

- **Set-up:** Who they are at the start and what they're trying to do?
- **Inciting incident:** What event leads to them having to act?
- **Commitment to the adventure:** Where there's no turning back without great consequences.

- **Midpoint:** What is their false victory/ defeat? What shows what winning/ losing could be like before it's complicated?
- **Devastation:** What is their moment of great loss?
- **One last try:** Changed by their moment of great loss, how do they push forward?
- **Confrontation:** The final confrontation.
- **Resolution:** The end, whether it's positive or negative.

Why this helps?

In looking at things through the eyes of the villain, you'll create motivation. Motivation in everyone is essential.

If you're stuck for a story to use, try one of these:

Jaws.
Star Wars: Episode IV - A New Hope.
The Lord of the Rings.
Misery.
The Matrix.
Die Hard.
Alien.
Cinderella.
James Bond: Casino Royale.

TAG TEAM

This exercise requires you to have fun with a friend or a group.

Your task:
Use one of the starting points coming up, or your own. Then:

- Create the characters.
- Take it in turns to write sentences for your story, ending each sentence with a "but", "so", or "however", so the next writer has to take over.
- Keep going until you run out of ideas.

Starting points:
You can amend these as you see fit.

- A teenage rebel arrives to meet an online friend at the shopping centre, but...

- A troubled parent searches their son's bedroom while they're out and finds a secret laptop, so...
- A pigeon learns to speak human, however...
- A mage sees their teacher being kidnapped, so...
- A newly married person sees their partner accepting an envelope of cash from their ex, but...
- A taxi driver is midway through driving a passenger to their destination when they realise they've died, so...
- An astronaut is forced to send data back to a rival country in exchange for the safety of their loved ones, however...

Why this helps?

Simple sentences can encapsulate drama, which will help you to improve your outline writing, structuring, and command of escalating stakes.

By doing this with others, you'll also experience another way of thinking, which can help you to see other solutions when you're problem solving.

It is messy, chaotic, and weird. That's the point. From the mess you might make something magical.

What this could look like:

I attempted this with my friend over text. To avoid overthinking, we had no more than five seconds to send the next message.

Here's what it looked like:

> A boy mage sees their annoying teacher being kidnapped from his boarding school, so...

> he goes into the teacher's office and...

steals their wallet, but...

> it's empty, apart from a glowing orb and mini carving of a wolf, however...

the wolf can talk, so...

> the mage asks what happened to the teacher, but...

the wolf bites the mage on the nose and runs away, however...

> as the mage gives chase, he runs into the teacher's wife, knocking ice cream onto her, so...

he apologises and says her husband was kidnapped by a goblin, but...

> she doesn't seem to care and hits on him, but...

he has just been dumped, so panics and runs to his room, however...

> the wolf is waiting for him and reveals he must find the mage, however...

the boy doesn't want to, because the teacher has always treated him badly, but...

> the wolf warns him that if he doesn't rescue his teacher by nightfall, then everyone will die...

It's an absolute mess and makes little sense, but we had fun, and there is a drama in there. A grumpy student who dislikes his teacher, but the teacher has some hidden life beyond the school.

There's a seemingly suspicious partner, an animal companion, and a mystery. So even in this chaos, I can find a story and feel inspired by some of what came out of a fun interaction.

DRAW THE POSTER

This solo exercise is about capturing the essence of your story and drawing. You do not have to be a good artist. It's about the meaning, not the execution.

Your task:

Take your film/book/TV series/play, whatever you're writing and draw the poster/front cover.

The aim is to capture the essence of your story in one image. How does it communicate tone and experience?

If you're struggling for inspiration, look online for existing film posters, book covers etc...

Why this helps?

This forces you to think of one powerful image that captures what your story is really about.

For example, the *Whiplash* poster has Andrew playing the drums with Fletcher hunched over shouting at him. That tells us everything the story is about and communicates tone. There's no sense of Andrew's girlfriend or family dynamics, because they're part of the character and story, but they're not the central drama.

STORY CORNER

This solo exercise requires you to write a short story, with the aim being that you start and finish something.
There is no set length for the story.

Your task:

- Write down the first object you think of.
- Write down the first profession you think of.
- Write down two opposing characteristics. For example, hard-working and lazy, or selfish and selfless.
- Write down the first location that you think of.
- Write a short story where your character has the profession you wrote, is in the location you chose, and in which the object plays a central role in them changing from one characteristic to the other.

Why this helps?

This forces you to finish something low-stakes, and also to use prompts as a guide. It also narrows focus early so you don't throw too many ideas into the arena.

By knowing which characteristic your protagonist starts with and which they end with, you can frame a narrative journey.

TIPS

If you're struggling in act two, it's because you have an issue in act one.

Your character is your structure.

It's easy to break something apart and analyse it. The art is in understanding people and what drives their actions.

Explore first, structure later.

Structure is the training wheels of writing. Character is the bike.

Use structure, don't abuse it.

Your protagonist is the foundation your structure is built upon.

Your structure and the emotional core of your story are tied together.

You can't break a story, so be bold, and save your old drafts.

Take writing day by day. Like a wall, it requires you to go brick by brick. If you only think of the finished product you'll exhaust yourself.

Follow where a story is going, rather than hanging on to where it has been.

If you're stuck, think about what the worst possible solution is. It can free your mind to find the best.

If your gut tells you something isn't right, listen.

RAISE THE STAKES

The most common notes a writer will receive are:

- The protagonist is inactive.
- This isn't delivering on genre.
- The character isn't likeable/relatable enough.
- The character's motivation isn't clear.
- The stakes aren't high enough.

The upcoming exercises aim to help you to raise the stakes and make them meaningful to your character. Then that note will disappear.

THE WORST THING THAT CAN HAPPEN

In this solo exercise you need to put your cruel hat on and embrace the role of punisher.

As storytellers, our job is to bring characters face to face with their worst fears. Look at *Get Out*. At one stage Chris learns his girlfriend has deceived him, he's in mortal danger, and is strapped to an armchair. That's as bad as it can get for him externally and internally. It also reflects on his feelings about his mother's death and his approach to life and love.

Your task:

1. Take your protagonist and spend ten minutes writing a list of ten of the worst things that can happen to them.
    - Think about what external events would crush them emotionally. What would make them feel so low they might not want to carry on doing what they're doing?
2. Once you've done that, choose one that feels the most connected to their transformative journey.

3. Write why it's the worst thing that can happen to them.

If you're struggling, think of the best thing that can happen to them and what that looks like, then think of the opposite.

Why this helps?
Sometimes we throw arbitrary obstacles and negative experiences at our characters in our attempts to create a story.

This exercise makes you create a low point that ties emotionally to your character, giving it more impact, and making the stakes higher.

External stakes are incredibly important, but the internal stakes connected to them create more impact, engagement, and satisfaction.

If you don't have a character, you can do the exercise on yourself.

GIVE IT MEANING

This solo exercise answers the question: 'What's my motivation?'

If actions aren't motivated, and if we don't know why somebody wants something, or it's not implied, then there's a disconnect, and a lack of internal stakes.

Writers should be able to make even the simplest thing matter if the story calls for it. For example, a character wanting a particular hat. Maybe the hat is a family heirloom that was stolen. Maybe the hat represents status that the protagonist is desperate for. Perhaps that hat is a reminder of their last memory with a parent who passed away wearing a similar one, and getting the hat will help the character deal with grief. I'm labouring the point, but things need to matter in order to sustain a story, whatever the genre.

Your task:

Use your protagonist, but if you haven't written one, do this on yourself:

- In the first person, write down your protagonist's goal.
- Write down the main reason it matters to them, and why.
- Keep asking why until there is something emotionally significant in the answer.

That's their true motivation and where it comes from, which enhances the meaning behind it.

Why this helps?

By knowing why a protagonist desperately wants to achieve what they want, you can communicate stakes.

The worst stories are when everything is too easy, so knowing why something means what it does to your protagonist allows you to create more tense obstacles, thus, raising the stakes.

Stories that lack stakes often don't establish them well enough at the beginning of the story.

THE POWER OF THE INCITING INCIDENT

This solo exercise focuses on the event that disrupts your protagonist's normality in the dramatic world. The inciting incident sets the story in motion and forces your protagonist to act.

This generally happens within the story, rather than off-screen/page, so we can feel the dramatic impact on your character.

It also sets the stakes. For example, in *Finding Nemo*, Nemo gets taken. Now Marlin could lose him forever, which forces him to venture into the ocean he wants nothing to do with.

Marlin believes being over-protective is best for keeping his son safe. He doesn't care that he holds Nemo back, and is in fact unaware of it. Nemo being taken is the worst thing that could happen, and as an inciting incident, is one that will truly test Marlin. It forces him to interact with a world he's avoided, which will both challenge and, at times reinforce his beliefs. He'll also learn to see his son in a new light. It has internal and external consequences and growth.

Also, we witness the inciting incident on screen. Imagine if the story starts with Marlin rushing around saying his son is missing, then off he goes into the ocean. It would lack the dramatic power of seeing it for ourselves.

Your task:

Create or use an existing protagonist:

- Write down the way they live life today and why?
- When you know why they behave the way they do, think of why that way of life may be detrimental to them.
- What do they need to engage with to shift perspective?
- Write a list of inciting incidents that would force them to take action in a way that they are not prepared for.

Why this helps?

This will help you to create emotionally impactful inciting incidents that tie to character and their psyche.

This helps you to see why whatever is happening externally has a deep internal impact. It shows you how success and failure carry huge emotional consequences.

THE CLOCK IS TICKING

This solo exercise looks at the usefulness of the ticking clock, which ramps up pressure in your story and gives your protagonist a limited amount of time to do something difficult and emotionally significant.

Take the film, *The Straight Story*, based on a true story. An old man, Alvin Straight, takes a journey across Iowa and Wisconsin on a lawn mower to see the brother he fell out with, who has had a stroke.

If he was just getting on his lawn mower to see his brother, it would be quirky and lovely, but undramatic. The fact his brother has had a serious health scare adds time stakes, and the fact they have fallen out creates even more pressure, because if he dies before they can reconcile, that's heartbreaking. It also means a lot of his journey reflects on family.

Whether it's a ticking clock over the entire story, part of it, or simply a scene, time pressure adds stakes.

These are examples of things that can add time pressure.

- A wedding.
- A job interview.
- A surgery.

- An election.
- A coronation.
- A funeral.
- An incoming disaster: earthquake, asteroid etc…
- A concert.
- Someone having to be home at a set time.

A ticking clock also adds suspense and poses questions depending on the context of the story. Will they make it? Will that person wait? Will they make enough money before the house is repossessed?

How many times in a romantic-comedy is there that scene where one person rushes to get to someone before they board a flight?

Suspense is dramatic and therefore engaging, and Alfred Hitchcock put it wonderfully:

"…Let's suppose that there is a bomb underneath this table between us. Nothing happens, and then all of a sudden, "Boom!" There's an explosion.

The public is surprised, but prior to this surprise, it has seen an absolutely ordinary scene, of no special consequence. Now, let us take a suspense situation.

The bomb is underneath the table and the public knows it, probably because they have seen the anarchist place it there. The public is aware the bomb is going to explode at one o'clock and there is a clock in the decor. The public can see that it is a quarter to one.

In these conditions, the same innocuous conversation becomes fascinating because the public is participating in the scene. The audience is longing to warn the characters on the screen: "You shouldn't be talking about such trivial matters. There is a bomb beneath you and it is about to explode!"

Your task:

Take one of the upcoming scenes or use your own, and add a ticking clock element to it.

Here are some examples you can use if you're not using a story you're working on:

- A former boxer trains for one last match.
- A young girl tries to return the bike she stole to the owner.
- A young woman wants to marry her boyfriend.
- An artist is desperate to finish a painting.
- A broken-hearted man wants to get back with his ex.
- A couple of friends try to decide where to scatter the ashes of their dead friend.
- A dying woman needs to decide what to do with her home and fortune when she dies.

Why this helps?

This helps you to see how you can raise the pressure, which in turn pushes your protagonist to their limit, tests them, and creates deeper emotional engagement.

We need to make things difficult, and a ticking clock can be a useful way to do that when it feels organic to your story.

What this could look like:

I'm intrigued by: *A young woman wants to marry her boyfriend.*

I think about why she might want to marry him. Obviously, because she loves him, but what if she wants to marry him because he has a terminal illness and he has always wanted to marry her, but she didn't believe in marriage? Or what if she's sick and wants to marry him, because it was her dream to get married? Or maybe there is parental pressure, or a financial need before a certain date? There are many routes we can take.

Then, once I've thought of a few, I'll think about which one interests me the most and can sustain a narrative. In some ways they all can. The financial one is really about how these people are wrong for each other, or maybe how they become right for each other under an initially cynical pretence. The one where she doesn't believe in marriage requires me to think about why she doesn't and what that journey will look like, and whether she would be so strong in her belief when he is dying. Maybe there's a twist where he's okay before the end and it makes them reconsider their relationship.

From these simple sentences you can expand on a life and find a potential story full of drama and high emotional stakes.

UP THE DRAMA

This solo or group exercise looks at the highs and lows of a story and increasing drama.

A story has emotional energy underneath every scene. Emotions for your characters and emotions for the audience.

Positivity shifts to negativity and vice versa. I've had a note in the past that a story didn't have enough ebb and flow. It was a story where a character was the victim of racism, and everything was miserable from that moment, which, while a fair reflection of the experience, was quite repetitive.

Your task:
Take three of these exceptionally bland scenes and make them dramatic. Consider the energy the scene starts with, and how it ends:

- A couple is at a restaurant for their anniversary meal. They eat it and it's great.
- A hired assassin has their target in sight, sneaks into a hotel and kills them.

- Two friends walk to school and arrive without any difficulty.
- Someone is in a job interview they're desperate for and they get the job.
- Someone wants a new jacket, and they get it.
- Someone goes to the meeting about their inheritance and gets lots of things they wanted.

It helps to think of a "but" as it creates opposition, conflict, and momentum.

Why this helps?

It allows you to look at a scene on a simple dramatic level. If this scene was placed next to others in a larger story, where would it fit dramatically? Would it serve a purpose to the story?

If you have a flat scene in your story, break it down to a simple sentence and see what the energy is. Is there a "but" or "however"? Does anything happen?

What this could look like:

In the one about the friends walking to school, I'm going to make them teenage friends, both from the same football team, one has a minor injury (Edwin), and the other is the one who accidentally injured him in training (Francis).

Then I think about how that can create complications in the bland sentence I provided. What if they have to run? What if some bullies chase them? What if a rival team sees them? What if one leaves the other behind? What if one confesses their love for the other's girlfriend, or for the friend?

My mind latches onto the idea of one leaving the other behind:

Two friends walk to school, but when a car chases them, one leaves the other behind.

If I wanted to develop it in more detail:

Francis walks to school with his friend Edwin and they playfully argue over who is the better striker and who should start for their team, when a car follows them. The boys run, but Edwin's injury slows him down, and Francis, rather than stopping to help him, leaves him behind.

That's dramatic. There's tension, energy, stakes, a decision, and emotion. You might think it's rubbish, but it's way better than what I presented to you, with a clear beginning, middle, and end.

BUT IT'S BORING

This solo exercise is similar to the last one, but approached from a different angle.

Your task:
Your goal is to take something boring to you and make it exciting, so:

1. Write down ten things that you find boring.
2. Write why they're boring to you.
3. Now write how you would make them exciting.
4. Choose one of the things you've written down and write a scene based on it.

Why this helps?
This will show you how you can inject drama and excitement into anything. Boring just means undramatic or uninteresting, and that's where your wonderful mind comes in.

It'll also help you to analyse why you find particular things boring.

TIPS

The stakes are low because nobody in your story cares about what's happening.

Our attachment to the story is your protagonist's attachment to their goal and why it matters to them.

Stakes are tied to emotions. If something has an emotional impact on your character, it matters.

What do you want more than anything in the world and why does it matter? That level of meaning is what your character needs in the story.

Think about how bad things can get. What would make it worse? And what would make it worse than that?

It's okay to be cruel to your characters to raise the stakes. They know what the job is.

TECHNIQUE AND GENERAL

There's a lot involved in crafting a story, from the creation and execution to the presentation.

I have found some writing students hate being given formatting notes, and they counter with: "If the story is good nobody will care."

There is an element of truth to that, but the story then has to be so good that the reader can forgive the errors.

Formatting and how you present your work shows a level of professionalism and love for your craft that goes a long way. It lets a reader know they're in safe hands, and in a job where people read multiple stories a day, sloppy errors jolt them out of the experience.

The upcoming exercises will help you to enhance your writing to create more pace, energy, and enjoyment. Some exercises will also touch upon subtext, visuals, and other essential tools.

The words you write matter.

DECLUTTERING

This solo exercise looks at pacing.

Nothing slows down a script or manuscript reading more than dense, repetitive blocks of text. In a first draft, don't worry, but before you send anything off, give it a polish to make sure every word earns its place.

With screen, it's often advised that no block of scene action exceed four lines unless it includes a character introduction. Think about where you can break it up.

Your task:

Below I have two passages. One is for a book, and one is for a script. Choose whichever applies to your discipline and cut out the clutter, or do both. You could decide to completely rewrite it.

Prose:

Fate had determined a clear hierarchy of status. At the top of Fate's list was Queen Val, obviously. She was a dominant, monstrous woman with a face as welcoming as a disturbed beehive. She was rumoured to have bitten the ears off one of her soldiers, just because she hated that they were more rounded than her own. It led to the current fad of long hair that swept through the kingdom, as people were desperate to hide their ears from her cruel gaze.

Screen:

Jon longingly stares at a board on his wall. Written on it are the following words to do with aspects of comedy: *Observations. Situations. Irony. Gross out. Deadpan. Farce. Slapstick. Personal. Cheesy puns. One Liners* is circled. Laura, not interested in what he's up to, walks in playing a game on her phone and slumps on her bed, ignoring Jon.

Why this helps:

We can slip into being too overt, when actions imply emotion.

Our job is to get the point across and keep the story moving. Words that don't add to the experience slow things down and create a disconnect.

There is a sense of voice that comes through in our words, so it's about balancing your voice with strong craft skills.

ACTIVATE

This solo exercise reminds us that as well as an active protagonist, we need to write using active language.

Active voice is when the subject performs the action. It's direct:

> John pushes a pram.

Passive voice is when the subject receives the action:

> A pram is pushed by John.

In screenwriting, for example, we often need to make changes around words ending "ing.":

> John is pushing a pram.

Becomes:

> John pushes a pram.

We also need to make our word choices dynamic. Rather than writing:

> Cindy runs really fast.

Use:

> Cindy sprints.

Reading a manuscript or a screenplay is an experience, and we control that experience through our choices.

Your task:

Choose three of the following. They're a mix of screenwriting and prose examples. Make them more active.

- Cinthia is looking at a coffee she craves.
- A donkey is being stroked by Edmundo.
- The car door is slammed by Tommy then he is seen walking angrily down the alleyway.
- The morgue was entered by Sandra, and a disappointed look was in her eyes.
- The salmon had been baked four hours ago by Costanza. Now, she served it nervously.
- Dominique, on her bicycle, is being chased by the police as she is riding it very quickly.

Why this helps?

This will help you to immerse your reader in your story. How often when reading or watching something does your attention drift to your phone or other thoughts? Your writing can help the person consuming your story to stay in the experience.

You'll also recognise how often you overwrite or undersell something.

ADD ESSENCE

This solo exercise is about how we describe our characters.

An issue I encounter in quite a few stories, is that people turn character descriptions into lists of insignificant physical traits. Physical traits are fine if the point of view character is observing them and commenting on them, as that reveals something of that POV character.

Another issue is when a character simply observes with no connection to who they are.

The key is to give a sense of the essence of a character. Here are some examples:

Screenwriting:
The Social Network: *MARK ZUCKERBERG is a sweet looking 19-year-old whose lack of any physically intimidating attributes masks a very complicated and dangerous anger. He has trouble making eye contact and sometimes it's hard to tell if he's talking to you or to himself.*

This works because it tells us what we see, and doesn't go

into hair type, chin size, or any nonsense we don't care about. It's fantastic in terms of tying physicality to the internal.

Prose:
The Girl on the Train: *"There is a pile of clothing on the side of the train tracks. Light-blue cloth - a shirt, perhaps - jumbled up with something dirty white. It's probably rubbish, part of a load fly-tipped into the scrubby little wood up the bank. It could have been something else. My mother used to tell me that I had an overactive imagination; Tom said that too. I can't help it, I catch sight of those discarded scraps, a dirty T-shirt or a lonesome shoe, and all I can think of is the other shoe, and the feet that fitted into them."*

Rachel's introduction tells us she's an observer, but an actively morbid one, and her internal voice reveals more than any immediate physical trait would.

It's up to you how you introduce your protagonist, but think about what you want the audience to think and feel. We can't guarantee they will, but we need to have intention. Audiences are building a profile from the first word.

Your task:
Write a character description that suggests who the person is, not just what they look like.

You can go the route of linking physical to psychological, or use the action they're doing to reveal something.

Think about where we meet them, what emotional state they're in, and why you want us to meet the protagonist this way.

Why this helps?
It makes you think about character more deeply and how

they may think and feel about themselves. It also makes you think about what is important to introduce now, and what you can reveal as the story progresses.

Strong character descriptions stay with the reader as the story progresses.

SUBTEXT

This solo or group exercise looks at the beauty of subtext.

Subtext is the meaning underneath what's being said. You can search online for great examples. It allows you to really get into someone's head.

It's rare people say exactly what they mean, unless they are that way inclined, as there are emotions and other factors that go into it. For example, if I've done something terrible and feel immense shame, it might be hard for me to say sorry, but I may do so in an action, because I'm too scared to look the person in the eye or say the words. I might even bring up a fond memory we shared, to rebuild some trust and connection.

There is a lot of power in actions, physicality, silence, and in the words that suggest something rather than directly addressing it.

Your task:

Take three of the challenges below and write a scene for each. Think of the people, the setting, and how they might express what they can't directly say.

- Someone says "I love you" without using the words.
- Someone says "I hate you" without using the words.
- Someone says "I forgive you" without using the words.
- Someone wants to ask to borrow money without saying it outright. They want the person to offer.
- Someone wants to reopen the discussion about having children with their partner without outright saying, "I want to talk about having kids."
- Someone wants to suggest killing their partner to a friend without saying it.
- Someone says "I'm lonely" without using the words.

Why this helps?

It makes you think about the characters, and often in later drafts of your work you'll start using more subtext, as the discovery draft is one where you're trying to get the story from A to B.

It also highlights the power of body language, character psychology, and meaning in action.

Let yourself experiment.

What this could look like:

I like the idea of showing loneliness without it being obviously stated, so I think about different reasons someone is lonely. Maybe they live alone. Or they have pushed everyone away. Maybe they're old and their friends have all passed away. Perhaps they have always been too busy at work to nurture friendships. Maybe they're eccentric so people avoid them.

I'm intrigued by the eccentric person, so I think about where they might live. Maybe they're in an apartment block, which adds to the loneliness, as even in a block full of people they have no connection.

I find myself leaning towards a sweet story, so this eccentric man decides to knock on a neighbours door. Being eccentric, it's not to borrow anything, but to get help resetting the date and time on his phone. He knows exactly how to do it, but it seemed the right way to get some engagement. Maybe as the neighbour helps he tries to start a conversation. Maybe the neighbour doesn't get the hint and the man will return the next day with the same problem. Maybe he'll pick up on the loneliness and invite him in. It also makes me think about who the neighbour is.

Once I decide what I think would be the most interesting, I'll write the scene. It could form part of a larger story about the power of friendship, and making connections no matter what stage of life we're in.

ONLY ACTION

This solo exercise is about silence, and you'll need a scene from an existing piece of work, whether it be yours or something you've seen/read.

Your task:
Take the scene and write it with no dialogue.

Why this helps?
This allows you to see how communicative we can be without dialogue. Dialogue is great, but some writers lean on it too much and forget the internal. Writing only action gets you into the internal world of your character.

BLURB IT OUT

This solo exercise will help you to face the tormenter of many writers - the blurb.

I can see why some people dislike writing blurbs. There are details and nuances we have to leave out to get to what the story is, and that can be a struggle for a lot of writers.

Your task:
Take any book, film, series, play you like. Then write a blurb for it.

Why this helps?
It forces you to concisely write a blurb for something that has already been through the rigour of multiple drafts and notes. In doing so, you'll notice how you leave out details to focus on the central drama.

You might combine act two beats into a sentence or paragraph as part of a journey, rather than getting into the minutiae of execution.

Doing this on existing work takes the pressure away, and lets you approach your own with a bit more ruthlessness when the time comes.

You can also do this for outlines if you struggle with those.

EXPOSITION

This solo exercise is about the joy of exposition and embracing it.

Some people treat exposition as a dirty word, but there is a lot that is wonderful about receiving information. The key is to do it creatively.

Look at *Star Wars: Episode IV - A New Hope*, it starts with a large exposition-dump of moving text, but it's atmospheric and pulls us into the story. It provides necessary context to ground the audience.

In the film version of *Dune*, Chani tells us what's going on while identifying key characters in the story, but to visuals that show the brutality and paint the world we're about to enter. It's creative context.

Exposition is about decisions. What is important to reveal now? What can be saved? And how should it be revealed?

Your task:

Take the following dialogue I have written between two people. There is no setting, action, or internal thoughts. Use your creativity to make it more engaging. You may decide to cut some of it, set it somewhere interesting, make it more specific, or have it happen during a particular action. Have fun with it and consider your genre and tone.

The conversation:
Mary: It's been three years.
Liam: I know.
Mary: Three years and all they have is a photo of him leaving a restaurant in Cyprus.
Liam: They're doing their best.
Mary: Their best is useless. People don't just disappear. Either they are made to, or they have a good reason to. They barely questioned anyone he was with on that trip. I'm going to go and look for him.
Liam: Is that a good idea? What about work, your family?
Mary: They'll understand.

Why this helps?
You'll see how you can reveal exposition more dramatically, and how setting and character dynamics can enhance its delivery.

It also makes you consider genre. In an action film, a lot of exposition is often delivered as asides in a tense action sequence, so there's movement, info, and energy everywhere.

Exposition is not a bad thing. It's about how we present it.

CLICHÉ AWAY

This solo or group exercise embraces the cliché. Clichés exist because they have worked before. It's about us putting a spin on them or subverting them.

The issue arises when they're used lazily. For example, take a road movie. How many times have we seen a car break down in a really tedious way just to slow people down and increase tension?

Your task:

Take a cliché. It can be one you are aware of, or one from this list:

- Road movie where a car breaks down.
- Horror jump scare.
- Romantic-comedy end of story chase scene where the person realises they've been stupid and has to get to the love of their life before it's too late.
- The villain's monologue where they explain everything while the hero is in peril.

- The creepy basement in a horror or cabin in the woods.

Now write an original version of that cliché. How can you subvert it? How can you put a twist on it and make it your own? How can you bring something new to the familiar? How can you completely discard it for something better?

Why this helps?

By spotting clichés, you can prevent your writing tipping into the obvious. It'll get you excited, thinking creatively, and show you how you can break from form. All clichés are there to elicit emotion, so what is the root emotion, and how can you create that in a unique way.

TIPS

Audiences love working things out, so give them enough to connect the dots for themselves.

Write with pride and passion. Those things transmit.

Never apologise for your work.

Nobody is out there looking for you, so contact people and share your work so that they are glad you found them.

It's the true imposters who don't have imposter syndrome.

It's not a bad thing if your first draft looks nothing like you imagined. It's a sign you're finding the true story.

Writing is a muscle you need to train.

Always have snacks nearby.

THE WRITER'S MIND

All of the following exercises should be done alone, as this section is about you.

Writing requires stamina, patience, a lot of talking to yourself, and juggling the different emotions that come with rejections, hope, opportunity, and growth.

There are often more downs than ups, and the downs are hard. But the ups, wow, when you have that creative breakthrough there's nothing like it.

I sometimes wonder why I write, because it is so difficult, and in some ways torturous, but for me, writing is what makes me who I am. There's no profound reason, there's no: "It helps me connect with the world," or fluffy soundbite. I just love creating, and I'm a better person when I do.

You'll hear people say that if you're good at something else, do it, because writing is a route to misery and poverty. However, I can't respect that advice, because it's too blunt and lacks nuance. It's more a case of, if you love writing, find a way to make it part of your life. Whether that's by working another job to pay the bills until writing fully sustains you, or by writing as a hobby. Do what works for you. I always ask people: "When you're on your death bed, what will you be glad you did?" Shut out the noise and listen to yourself.

I hope the exercises around mental health help you to remember why you do this.

Some of these could be used on your characters to discover more about them.

WHAT'S THE BEST THAT CAN HAPPEN?

Writers are good at leaning into catastrophe. It's the job. However, that sadly comes with consequences where we can look at our work and ourselves catastrophically when it's not going so well.

Your task:

Write all of the amazing things that could happen as a result of you finishing your story. Spend fifteen minutes doing it. For example:

- Maybe it'll sell loads and be a hit.
- Maybe it'll help someone with something they're struggling with.
- Maybe it'll inspire someone.
- What if someone tells you how much it cheered them up or changed their life?
- What if someone makes fan art about it?
- Maybe you'll love the story again and be proud of it once you've finished.

- What if it leads to someone you admire wanting to work with you?
- What if it makes you a better writer?

Now go back through each one and really visualise it in your mind. Live the moment. Which is the one that really hit you? Did one give you goosebumps?

Write it down and put it near your computer as a reminder.

Why this helps?

Looking at the positive will shake away the negative thoughts that are stopping you writing.

Focusing on the good that can come of it could lift you out of any slump, and writing things down makes them more real.

LETTER TO YOURSELF

People often talk about what they would say to their 14-year-old self. But I don't care for looking back. I think it's important to play with looking forward.

Your task:
Go back to being your 14-year-old self, or younger if that feels more meaningful. What would you say to the older version of yourself with the knowledge you have, to keep yourself writing?

What would they be amazed by, not only in your writing, but in how you live your life?

Maybe they're in awe that you can do three press-ups now and that you eat vegetables. Maybe they are so proud you moved out or rebuilt yourself after that terrible relationship. Maybe they are thrilled that you wrote your first line.

Why this helps?
When we're in a low, it's hard to see the little wins. By looking through your younger self's eyes at the good things that

have happened, you'll remember things you've forgotten in the haze of the writing struggle.

To your younger self, some of the things you now don't see as so big are huge. It's important to look at life through the eyes of curiosity, ambition, and hopefulness that comes with everything being on the horizon.

We're so trained to focus on what's next we forget to love how far we've come.

When you've written this letter, keep it somewhere to look at from time to time.

Variation:

If you're a younger reader, you can do the version where you write a letter to the older version of you.

NO TO YOUR NOTES

Notes...
There's no escaping notes. Some are wonderful, some are downright unbearable and nonsensical.

What's important is to never reply to them immediately. Read, be angry, process, then say thank you and deal with the ones that are useful. Sometimes we want to vent, and this exercise is designed for that.

Your task:
When you receive annoying notes, write the email you wish you could send. Unfiltered, direct, confrontational, overly nice if that's your approach. Whatever you want to say that you don't feel you can, do it, but for the love of all that is decent remove their name from the sender list before you type even one word.

Have fun with it. Let yourself go.

Why this helps?
Venting is important, but it's also really ungrateful at times. The reason we don't vent at the person giving us notes is

because we don't want to get fired, but also deep down we know there is some value somewhere in their word weeds. Also, they made the effort to read our work.

By writing what you wish you could, you'll playfully engage with the negative, and you'll diffuse it. You'll process it in a fun way and move on sooner.

Sometimes, rather than being stuck in our own minds, writing things out can be a release.

I LOVE WRITING BECAUSE...

Your task:
Spend ten minutes writing down all the reasons you love writing. Don't stop during that ten minutes, or edit. Write everything down, no matter how silly or serious.

Why this helps?
It's easy to fall into a negative mindset, so writing down all the weird and wonderful reasons we love writing can rebalance us and help us to rediscover enthusiasm.

I'M ALLOWED TO...

It's easy to feel guilty for not doing something, and we live in a time where everyone is seemingly endlessly productive, or proud of how busy they are, even if it means their health suffers.

Your task:

Write a list of things you're allowed to do that you may normally feel guilty about. For example:

- I'm allowed to play video games.
- I'm allowed to not write for a day.
- I'm allowed to buy myself that hat that makes my head look less like a peanut.

You get it.

Why this helps?

The two greatest routes to misery are perfectionism and shame.

This turns your writing space into a safe place and makes you realise some of the dumb rules you're following subconsciously that add pressure.

Give yourself permission to exist outside of writing. The world is where inspiration is, and you're not a machine. Perfectionism can invade every area of your day, so lean into being imperfect. It's what makes you human and wonderful.

MAKE A VOW

It's easy to get lost when you have lots going on. And sometimes we try to achieve too much. We're often told to simplify our stories, and we also need to simplify our lives. So, we're going to make a vow.

Your task:

- Write a vow on what you will do in the next six months as a writer. One thing. It can be to finish a story, or to simply read a book.
- Write it down on paper and stick it somewhere you can see it every day.
- Look at it and think about why it matters to you to achieve it.
- Visualise yourself achieving it and what that will feel like.

Why this helps?

By committing to one thing, you will declutter your mind, and by placing your goal somewhere you can see it daily you'll remind yourself to visualise it.

This keeps you focused.

WHAT'S STOPPING ME?

Time and responsibility, the biggest impediments to writing. Kids, jobs, bills, health, the list could go on. However, if you really want to do it you need to find a way to fit writing into your life.

The issue comes when you put the pressure on writing time to be perfect. It stops you ever starting because you're already thinking the worst.

This should hopefully help.

Your task:

You're going to identify what is getting in your way and then come up with a plan.

Step one:

Write a list of all the things that are stopping you from writing, from the serious to the small. Go beneath the surface.

For example, when I was struggling to write, the things that were getting in my way were my job, my drinking issues, and my fear of failure, which is where the drinking issues and doing a job I didn't enjoy came from.

Do spend time on this. It'll be difficult, but eye-opening.

Write down why each of these things prevents you writing.

Step two:

Go through your list, and write down how you can deal with the issue. For example, if I go out too much, then of course, one less night a week is an action. If I have a young child, then my action is to organise a small amount of time I can have to write, if that means leaning on my partner or a family member.

It's about a healthy balance.

Now take action:

- Cut the bad habits.
- Work around the things that are hard to avoid, like parenting, work, health issues, or being someone's carer.
- Set aside small blocks of writing time, where even if you're not in the mood you turn up. Fifteen minutes a day to start with.

Writing is about discipline, and small changes. You'll never go from zero writing time to all the writing time for any prolonged period, so give yourself small goals. If you have fifteen minutes and write nothing, you still turned up and thought about it. Allow the habit to build.

Sadly, yes, there are things that get in the way, but the main obstacle is us.

TIPS

Writing is incredibly brave. Be proud of yourself.

Put the love in, and you'll get it back, maybe not in external results, but definitely in internal growth.

Nobody can write the way you do. Don't dilute your voice.

Write out your five favourite things about writing and stick them above your workspace.

The greatest gift is the time to create.

Productivity doesn't only live on the page. It's in our growth as writers and people.

The best writers are the ones who stick around long enough.

You only fail when you stop trying.

Sharing a story is sharing a piece of yourself.

Stop refreshing your emails.

Prioritise what you care about.

Be still. Nothing good comes from rushing around.

Rather than thinking about what happens if you fail, think about what happens when you succeed.

It's okay to step away when you're feeling overwhelmed.

Have a small group of trusted readers who will give you honest feedback, but who also understand what you're trying to do.

You are part of the package, not just your story. Be proud of your work, what you've achieved, and who you are. The person listening wants to feel your passion.

It's okay to not have all the answers. They'll come as you explore, then you'll have new questions to answer.

That story you love went through hundreds of drafts. Don't judge your first draft against someone's final draft.

THE FINAL CHALLENGE

By now you will have hopefully done some of the exercises. If you've done all of them, then honestly, you're a superhuman and I want to be like you.

But I have one final challenge for you...

YOUR TIME TO SHINE

Hopefully you've seen the benefit of play and engaged your creative side. However, like many good stories there's a twist, and now I throw the pen to you for your graduation exercise.

Your task:
Create a writing exercise. It can be anything. Remember, there's verbal, physical, words, sounds. Anything. Be free and have fun.

Why this helps?
By now I shouldn't need to tell you why this helps. Go. Live. Write.

BIBLIOGRAPHY

Films:

Alien (1979). Directed by Ridley Scott. Written by Dan O'Bannon. 20th Century Fox, Brandywine Productions

Birdemic: Shock and Terror (2008). Directed and written by James Nguyen. Moviehead Pictures.

Die Hard (1988). Directed by John McTiernan. Written by Jeb Stuart and Steven E. de Souza. Based on the novel *Nothing Lasts Forever* by Roderick Thorp. 20th Century Fox.

Dune (2021). Directed by Denis Villeneuve. Written by Jon Spaihts, Denis Villeneuve, Eric Roth. Legendary Pictures.

Finding Nemo (2003). Directed by Andrew Stanton. Written by Bob Peterson, David Reynolds, and Andrew Stanton. Walt Disney Pictures and Pixar Animation Studios

Get Out (2017). Directed and written by Jordan Peele. Blumhouse Productions.

Hard Ticket to Hawaii (1987). Directed and written by Andy Sidaris. Malibu Bay Films.

James Bond: Casino Royale (2006). Directed by Martin Campbell. Written by Neal Purvis, Robert Wade and Paul Haggis. Based on the novel by Ian Fleming. Eon Productions.

Jaws (1975). Directed by Steven Spielberg. Written by Peter Benchley and Carl Gottlieb. Universal Pictures.

Star Wars: Episode IV - A New Hope (1977). Directed and written by George Lucas. Lucasfilm.

The Matrix (1999). Directed and written by Lana Wachowski and Lilly Wachowski. Warner Bros. Pictures.

The Room (2003). Directed and written by Tommy Wiseau. Wiseau-Films.

The Social Network (2010). Directed by David Fincher. Written by Aaron Sorkin. Columbia Pictures, Relativity Media, Scott Rudin Productions, Michael De Luca Productions, Trigger Street Productions

The Straight Story (1999). Directed by David Lynch. Written by John Roach and Mary Sweeney. Asymmetrical Productions, Canal+, FilmFour, Ciby 2000, Le Studio Canal+

Troll 2 (1990). Directed and written by Claudio Fragasso. Filmirage.

Whiplash (2014). Directed and written by Damien Chazelle. Bold Films, Blumhouse Productions, Right of Way Films.

Books:

Aristotle, *The Poetics* (Penguin Classics, 1996)

Brown, Stuart and Vaughan, Christopher, *Play: How it Shapes the Brain, Opens the Imagination, and Invigorates the Soul* (Penguin Publishing Group, 2010)

Boutros, Mark, *The Craft of Character* (Mark Boutros, 2020)

Hawkins, Paula, *The Girl on the Train* (Doubleday, 2015)

King, Stephen, *Misery* (Viking Press, 1987)

Perrault, Charles, *Cinderella* (Originally published in *Histoires ou contes du temps passé,* Paris: Claude Barbin, 1697)

Tolkien, J.R.R, *The Lord of the Rings* (George Allen and Unwin, 1954)

Truffaut, Francois, *Hitchcock* (Flamingo, 1978)

Vogler, Christopher, *The Writer's Journey: Mythic Structure for Writers* (Michael Wiese Productions, 2007)

TV:

30 Rock (2006). Created by Tina Fey. Broadway Video. Little Stranger, Inc. Universal Television.

Friends (1994-2004). Created by David Crane and Marta Kauffman. Bright/Kauffman/Crane Productions. Warner Bros. Television.
Friends. The One With The Cop. Season 5 Episode 16. NBC. 25th February 1999.

Money Heist (2017). Created by Álex Pina. Atresmedia. Vancouver Media.

Schitt's Creek (2015). Created by Eugene Levy and Daniel Levy. Not a Real Company Productions. Canadian Broadcasting Corporation. Pop Media Group.

Ted Lasso (2020). Developed by Jason Sudekis, Bill Lawrence, Brendan Hunt, Joe Kelly. Ruby's Tuna Inc. Doozer. Universal Television. Warner Bros. Television.

ACKNOWLEDGMENTS

Everyone likes being acknowledged. So here we are...

First, a massive thank you to all my students. They make my job the most rewarding one I've ever had. Teaching is a real privilege, and despite the poor pay, it's something I will do until I no longer can.

The writers I meet every year ask incredible questions, challenge ideas, and share their creativity with such bravery. I am full of admiration for them, and they inspired me to write this book. Without their engagement I wouldn't have bothered.

A big thank you goes to Adam Croft, best-selling crime thriller author. He did absolutely nothing, but he needs thanks or he gets sad.

I also want to thank my advanced readers, especially Júlia Gispert, Natalia Ramirez Gil, and Melanie Jill, who found so many sloppy errors, and road-tested a lot of the exercises. Their attention to detail is phenomenal, and I can't wait to read their work. Their honesty and encouragement was truly motivating.

A huge thanks goes to Matthew McMillion, a brilliant editor and teacher who gave me great ideas on how to enhance some of the exercises to make them even more useful to you. He suggested I have the sections on how the exercises could look, which was a wonderful piece of advice.

A very big thank you goes to Christelle Roy-Corbin. I sent her an advanced copy for feedback, and she did way more by doing a brilliant full edit which left me no choice but to offer her an editor credit. She is awesome, and it highlights what a wonderfully passionate community we have.

A huge thanks goes to you, the readers. I don't get to do anything without your support and feedback. I'll keep trying to be useful and you can tell me when I'm not.

And my final, biggest thanks goes to my wife, Cinthia. She is the most interesting and encouraging human I've ever met. Her curiosity inspires me and she has listened to me ramble through so many ideas. I owe her everything. I hope our daughter takes after her.

To everyone, keep writing, learning, and pursuing what you care about. The world is much nicer when you find time to do what you love.

ABOUT THE AUTHOR

Mark Boutros is an International Emmy nominated screenwriter, hybrid author, story consultant and writing teacher with a passion for helping writers to craft compelling characters and emotionally resonant stories.

With a background in comedy and TV, his work has been broadcast on the BBC, Sky One, Sky Arts and more. He is the author of *The Craft of Character*, and the *Karl's Kingdom* series.

He also runs a writing consultancy and school with brilliant BAFTA nominated writer, director, author, and performer, Nat Luurtsema. You can see more at www.workingwriters.co.uk

When he's not writing or teaching, he's probably overthinking the emotional arc of a talking animal.

You can find more of his books at www.mark-boutros.com/book-library

And you can join the mailing list at: www.mark-boutros.com/blog

    instagram.com/storydork
    facebook.com/MarkBoutrosWrites
    tiktok.com/@story_dork

www.ingramcontent.com/pod-product-compliance
Lightning Source LLC
Chambersburg PA
CBHW052030070526
44584CB00016B/1975